Colours in Nature

KT-523-576

Green

Lisa Bruce

Little Nippers

www.heinemann.co.uk/library
Visit our website to find out more information about **Heinemann Library** books.

To order:
☎ Phone 44 (0) 1865 888066
▤ Send a fax to 44 (0) 1865 314091
▭ Visit the Heinemann Bookshop at www.heinemann.co.uk/library to browse our catalogue and order online.

First published in Great Britain by Heinemann Library, Halley Court, Jordan Hill, Oxford OX2 8EJ, part of Harcourt Education. Heinemann is a registered trademark of Harcourt Education Ltd.

Editorial: Jilly Attwood and Claire Throp
Design: Jo Hinton-Malivoire and bigtop, Bicester, UK
Models made by: Jo Brooker
Picture Research: Catherine Bevan
Production: Severine Ribierre

Originated by Dot Gradations
Printed and bound in China by South China Printing Company

ISBN 0 431 17232 3 (hardback)
07 06 05 04 03
10 9 8 7 6 5 4 3 2 1

ISBN 0 431 17237 4 (paperback)
07 06 05 04 03
10 9 8 7 6 5 4 3 2 1

British Library Cataloguing in Publication Data
Bruce, Lisa
Green – (Colours in nature)
535.6
A full catalogue record for this book is available from the British Library.

Acknowledgements
The publishers would like to thank the following for permission to reproduce photographs:
Ardea pp. 8-9 (Iam Beames), **18-19** (Francois Gohier); Bruce Coleman p. **12-13** (John Cancalosi); Digital Vision p. **14-15**; Imagestate pp. **16**, **17**; John Walmsley p. **6**; Robert Harding p. **7**; SPL pp. **4-5** (Pat & Tom Leeson), **10** (Hermann Eisenbeiss), **11** (left) (Gusto), **11** (top right) (Jeremy Burgess), **11** (bottom right) (Gusto), **20-21** (Damien Lovegrove), **21** (right) (Acestock/David Solzberg), **22-23** (John Heseltine)

Cover photograph reproduced with permission of SPL/Hermann Eisenbeiss

The publishers would like to thank Annie Davy for her assistance in the preparation of this book.

Every effort has been made to contact copyright holders of any material reproduced in this book. Any omissions will be rectified in subsequent printings if notice is given to the publishers.

2

Contents

Green in nature

Nature is full of wonderful colours.

What can you think of
in nature that is green?

Green grass

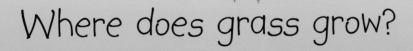

Where does grass grow?

Green Snakes

Ssss

Slowly, silently, the snake **slithers** through the grass.

9

Green leaves

Leaves come in different shapes and sizes.

There are lots of shades of green too.

Green insects

Some insects are green so that they can hide in the leaves. Can you see the cricket?

13

Green caterpillar

Creeping, crawling
along the ground.
First it goes up,
then it goes down.

15

Do you know who is hiding
under the water lily?

16

A green frog!

ribbit!

17

Green birds

Some of the most colourful birds in the world are parrots.

Can you see their long green tail feathers?

Squawk!

Green food

Gooseberries

Broccoli

Courgettes

Which green foods do you like best?

Brussels sprouts

Grapes

Cabbage

Changing colour

Leaves change colour in the autumn.

22

At first they are green.
What colours do they change to?

Index

The end

Notes for adults

This series supports young children's knowledge and understanding of the world around them. The four books will help to form the foundation for later work in science and geography. The following Early Learning Goals are relevant to this series:
• begin to differentiate colours
• explore what happens when they mix colours
• find out about and identify some features of living things, objects and events they observe
• look closely at similarities, differences, patterns and change
• ask questions about why things happen and how things work
• observe, find out about and identify features in the places they live and the natural world
• find out about their environment, and talk about those features they like and dislike.

The Colours in Nature series introduces children to colours and their different shades by exploring features of the natural world. It will also help children to think more about living things and life processes, which may lead on to a discussion of environmental issues. The children should be encouraged to be aware of the weather and seasonal changes and how these affect the place in which they live.

This book will help children extend their vocabulary, as they will hear new words such as snake, insects, cricket, parrots, gooseberries, courgettes and broccoli.

Additional information
The cricket is an insect related to the grasshopper and katydid. It is known for the loud chirping noises they make by rubbing their wing casings against their hind legs. Caterpillars do not breathe through their mouths. Air enters their bodies through a series of small tubes along the sides of their thorax and abdomen. Rather than having fully-developed eyes, they have six eyelets on the lower part of their head. They rely on their antennae to help them locate food.

Follow-up activities
Collect leaves from various trees or shrubs. Stick these onto paper to make a collage and discuss their different sizes, shapes, textures and colours. Encourage children to use descriptive words such as spiky, shiny, thin, stripy, smooth or rough while talking about the leaves.

Sing nursery rhymes with a green theme such as 'Green grow the rushes-O' and 'Here we go round the mulberry bush'.